Toto & Lola

FRENCH

FOR KIDS

ALPHABET   NUMBERS   COLORS

© Copyright 2018 Imane Diouri

In the same collection:

Book 1: Alphabet, Numbers, Colors

Book 2: Days of the week, Months, Seasons

Book 3: Family, Clothes, Time

Also available in Spanish and Italian!

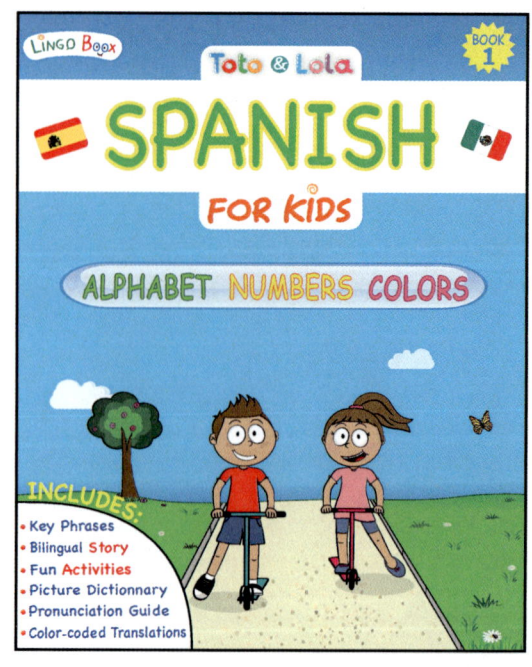

Bonjour and welcome to the world of Toto & Lola !

Teaching your child a second language is one of the best gift you can offer and Toto and Lola want to help!

This book was designed for beginners with short and easy to understand phrases and no tedious grammar lessons.

Each sentence comes with its translation and pronunciation guide if you are not (yet!) fluent in French or for children who are reading on their own. You will also find extra pronunciation tips at the end of the book to get your child speaking as a true French!

Following the story, a few fun activities will help reinforce memorization and test your child's progress.
You can also find free printable worksheets to accompany this book on www.lingoboox.com.

Repetition is key when learning a language: **short, frequent repetitions (15 minutes a day) are more effective than a one hour lesson once a week.**
<u>**A daily dose of French is the key to success!**</u>

This book is part of a series so keep an eye out for more adventures with Toto and Lola.

Learning French is exciting and we are thrilled to be part of your child's foreign language journey!

Alors, commençons!

L'ALPHABET
(lahl·fah·beh)

A ah	**B** beh	**C** seh	**D** deh	**E** uh
F ef	**G** zheh[1]	**H** ash	**I** ee	**J** zhee[1]
K kah	**L** el	**M** em	**N** en	**O** oh
P peh	**Q** qew	**R** air	**S** ess	**T** teh
U ew[2]	**V** veh	**W** doobl-veh	**X** eeks	**Y** ee-grehk
Z zed				

([1] zh sounds like "si" in vision)

([2] make an "O" shape with your lips while saying "ee")

ORANGE

oh-r<u>ah</u>n<u>zh</u>*

ORANGE

LES COULEURS

(leh coo-luhr)

-COLORS-

NOIR

nwahr

BLACK

BLEU

bluh

BLUE

BLANC

bl<u>ahn</u> *

WHITE

ROUGE

roozh

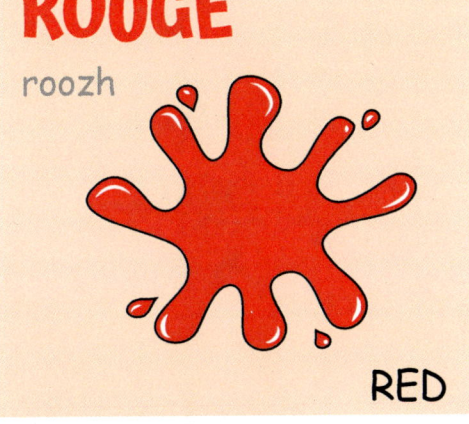

RED

VERT

vehr

GREEN

ROSE

roz

PINK

MARRON

mahr-<u>ohn</u>*

BROWN

JAUNE

zhohn

YELLOW

GRIS

gree

GREY

VIOLET

veeo-leh

PURPLE

*nasal sound- "n" not pronounced

5

Let's count to 20!

0 zero
(zeh-roh)

1 un
(<u>u</u>hn)*

2 deux
(duh)

3 trois
(trwah)

4 quatre
(kah·tr)

5 cinq
(sank)

6 six
(sees)

7 sept
(set)

8 huit
(weet)

9 neuf
(nuhf)

10 dix
(dees)

11 onze
(<u>Ohn</u>z)*

12 douze
(dooz)

13 treize
(trez)

14 quatorze
(kah·torz)

15 quinze
(k<u>ahn</u>z)*

16 seize
(sez)

17 dix-sept
(dees·set)

18 dix-huit
(dees·weet)

19 dix-neuf
(dees·nuhf)

20 vingt
(v<u>Ahn</u>)*

BRAVO!

* nasal sound - <u>hn</u> not pronounced

7

LE BALLON
luh bah•<u>lohn</u>*

the ball

LA TROTTINETTE
la troh•tee•net

the scooter

LE CHÂTEAU DE SABLE
luh shah•toh duh sah•bluh

the sandcastle

LE SCEAU
luh soh

the bucket

LA BILLE
la bee•yuh

the marble

L'ARBRE
lahr•bruh

the tree

LA FLEUR
la fluhr

the flower

LA COCCINELLE
la coh•ksee•nel

the ladybug

LA FEUILLE
la fuh•yuh

the leaf

LA PIERRE
la pee•yehr

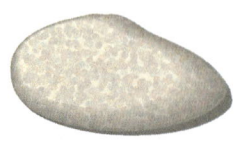

the rock

L'OISEAU
lwah•zoh

the bird

LE BANC
luh b<u>ahn</u>*

the bench

8

* nasal sound - "n" not pronounced

L'ASSIETTE
lahs•yet

the plate

LE RAISIN
luh reh•zahn*

the grape

LA MYRTILLE
la meer•tee

the blueberry

LE BISCUIT
luh bees•kwee

the cookie

LE DOIGT
luh dwah

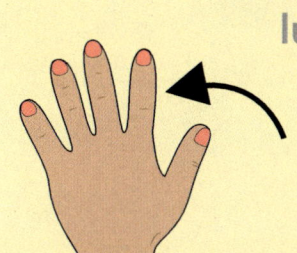

the finger

LA MAIN
la mahn*

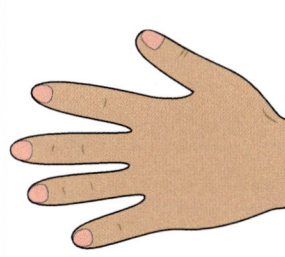

the hand

LA CLEF
la cleh

the key

LA PIÈCE
la pee•yes

the coin

LE PANIER
luh pah•nyeh

the basket

Great job!
Now let's find these
words in the story!

⚠ All nouns in French have a
gender (masc. or fem). The article
(the) will vary depending on the
gender (m./f.) and number (sing./plur.)
Le = the (masc.) *e.g: le panier* (luh pah•nyeh)
La = the (fem.) *e.g: la cléf* (lah cleh)
Les = the (plural) (masc. or fem.)
e.g: les paniers, les cléfs (leh pah•nyeh , leh cleh)

Au parc

At the park (oh park)

Toto

Lola

CoCo

A little "coccinelle" 🐞 is following Toto and Lola!
It is hiding in every picture of the story. Can you spot it?

zhay[1] uhn[2] bah·lohn[2] nwahr eh blahn[2]

J'ai un ballon noir et blanc.

I have one black and white ball.

· · · · · · · ·

zhuh[1] teer eh tew ah·trahp

Je tire et tu attrapes!

I kick and you catch!

Now repeat these words

1 UN · BALLON* · NOIR · BLANC

REMEMBER:

- [1] "zh" sounds as the s in "treasure"

- Nouns have a gender, they are either feminine or masculine

- [2] hn not pronounced, indicates a nasal sound See p.29

- *Can also be called "une balle". ewn bahl

11

fuh•zohn lah coors ah•vehk noh duh tro•tee•net

Faisons la course avec nos deux trottinettes.

Let's race with our two scooters.

• • • • • • • •

rohz oo oh•rahnzh kee ah gah•nyeh coco sewr sohn sket-bord

Rose ou orange? Qui a gagné? Coco sur son skateboard!

Pink or orange? Who won? Coco on his skateboard!

2 DEUX   TROTTINETTE   ORANGE   ROSE

12

ruh•gahr•duh eeleeyah trwah coh•ksee•nel roozh

Regardes! Il y a trois coccinelles rouge!

Look! There are three red ladybugs!

• • • • • • • •

el sohn sewr set fluhr vee•oh•let

Elles sont sur cette fleur violette.*

They are on this purple flower.

REMEMBER:

- In French, most adjectives follow the noun.

- They also agree with the noun in gender and number
e.g. :
* violet (masc.)
(vee•yoh•leh)

violette (fem.)
(vee•yo•let)

violettes (fem.
(vee•yo•let) plur.)

3
TROIS COCCINELLE FLEUR ROUGE VIOLET*

13

noo fuh·zohn kahtr shah·toh duh sah·bluh ah·vec luh soh zhoh·nuh

Nous faisons quatre châteaux de sable avec le sceau jaune.

We make four sandcastles with the yellow bucket.

● ● ● ● ● ● ● ●

oh oh coco vuh noo·zeh·deh

Oh oh! Coco veut nous aider...

Oh oh! Coco wants to help us...

REMEMBER:

● The word ending -*eau* makes the sound "oh"
e.g.:
-sceau (soh)

● For plural nouns, add an -s except with nouns ending in -au and -eau, add -x instead:
e.g.: - ballons
      - chateaux
      - sceaux

| 4 QUATRE | CHATEAU DE SABLE | JAUNE | SCEAU |

Moi !*

*Moi (mwah) = me

pruh•nohn ewn pohz duh sank mee•newt

Prenons une pause de cinq minutes.

Let's take a break of five minutes.

• • • • • • • •

oov•ruh luh pah•nyeh mah•rohn kee vuh mahn•zheh

Ouvres le panier marron. Qui veut manger?

Open the brown basket. Who wants to eat?

5 CINQ   PANIER   BROWN

15

Eeleeyah see puh•tee bees•kwee sewr las•yet bluh

Il y a <u>six</u> petits biscuits sur l'assiette bleue.

There are six little cookies on the blue plate.

• • • • • • • •

zhuh vwah ewn paht   kee vuh <u>uhn</u> bees•kwee

Je vois une patte... Qui veut un biscuit?

I see a paw... Who wants a cookie?

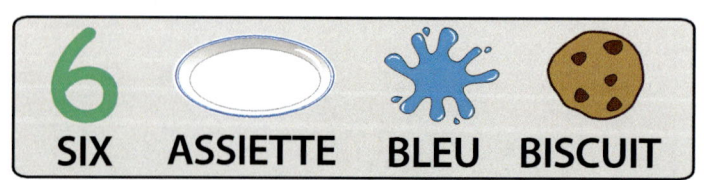

6 SIX   ASSIETTE   BLEU   BISCUIT

ruh•gahrd　　leh　frwee　sewr　m<u>ohn</u>　ahs•yet　　soo-ree

Regardes! Les fruits sur mon assiette sourient!

Look! The fruits on my plate are smiling!

• • • • • • • •

zhe m<u>ahn</u>•zhe set　reh•z<u>ahn</u>　vehr　eh　weet　meer•tee

Je mange sept raisins verts et huit myrtilles.

I eat seven green grapes and eight blueberries.

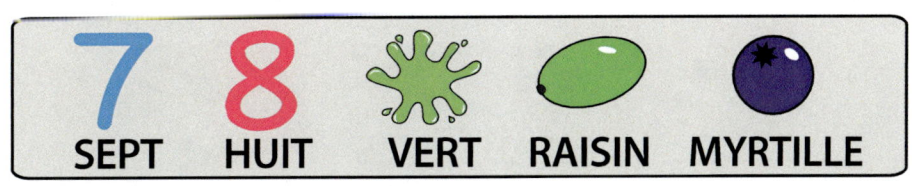

7	8			
SEPT	HUIT	VERT	RAISIN	MYRTILLE

nuhf   wah·zoh   gree   m<u>ahn</u>·zhuh   noh   grehn

Neuf oiseaux gris mangent nos graines!

Nine grey birds eat our seeds!

• • • • • • • •

coco   poor·kwah   eh   tew   dehr·yehr   luh   b<u>ahn</u>

Coco, pourquoi es–tu derrière le banc?

Coco, why are you behind the bench?

9	🕊	💦	🪑
NEUF	**OISEAU**	**GRIS**	**BANC**

Ruh•gardeh meh m<u>ah</u>n comb•y<u>ah</u>n duh dwah vwah•yeh voo

Regardez mes mains. Combien de doigts voyez-vous?

Look at my hands. How many fingers do you see?

• • • • • • • •

noo par•t<u>oh</u>n d<u>ah</u>n dee mee•newt ah <u>ohn</u>z uhr

Nous partons dans dix minutes. A onze heures.

We leave in ten minutes. At eleven o'clock.

Litterally "heures" means "hours"

19

ohn shehr•sh deh treh•zor   kah tew troo•veh Lola

On cherche des trésors! Qu'as-tu trouvé Lola?

We look for treasures! What did you find Lola?

• • • • • • • •

zheh troo•veh dooz cleh trehz fluhr eh kah•torz pee•yes

J'ai trouvé douze cléfs, treize fleurs et quatorze pièces.

I found twelve keys, thirteen flowers and fourteen coins!

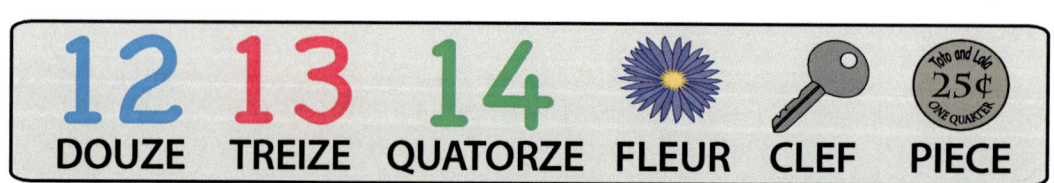

12	13	14			
DOUZE	TREIZE	QUATORZE	FLEUR	CLEF	PIECE

20

eh mwah zheh k<u>ah</u>nz pee•yehr sehz fuh•yuh

Et moi, j'ai quinze pierres, seize feuilles...

And (me), I have fifteen rocks, sixteen leaves...

• • • • • • • •

eh dee•set bee•yuh kehl sh<u>ah</u>ns

and dix–sept billes! Quelle chance!

and seventeen marbles! How lucky!

REMEMBER:

- In French, the plural ending -s or -x are not pronounced

15	16	17			
QUINZE	SEIZE	DIX-SEPT	PIERRE	BILLE	FEUILLE

21

zhoo•<u>ohn</u> ah kash•kash zhuh c<u>oh</u>nt dehr•yehr lahr•bruh

Jouons à cache-cache! Je compte derrière l'arbre,

Let's play (at) hide and seek! I count behind the tree,

• • • • • • • •

eh tew tuh kash deez•weet deez-nuhf v<u>ah</u>n zhah•reev

et tu te caches. Dix-huit, dix-neuf, vingt! J'arrive!*

and you hide. Eighteen, nineteen, twenty! Here I come!

18	19	20
DIX-HUIT	DIX-NEUF	VINGT

22

*litteraly: "I arrive"

Let's play!

NUMBER SCRAMBLE!

COLOR FINDER

SPOT IT

NUMBER SCRAMBLE!

Silly Toto! He mixed up all the numbers for Hide and Seek! Match each word to its matching number in the picture to put them back in the right order.

UN	DEUX	TROIS	QUATRE	CINQ
SIX	SEPT	HUIT	NEUF	DIX
ONZE	DOUZE	TREIZE	QUATORZE	QUINZE
SEIZE	DIX-SEPT	DIX-HUIT	DIX-NEUF	VINGT

COLOR FINDER

Complete the sentences with the correct colors:

Les fleurs sont ___ et ___ .

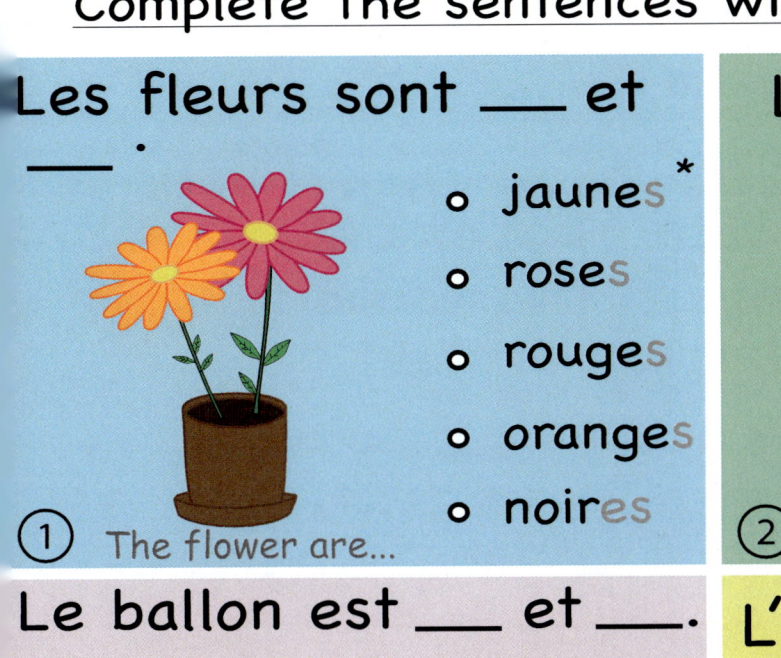

- o jaunes*
- o roses
- o rouges
- o oranges
- o noires

① The flower are...

L'oiseau est ___ .

- o vert
- o rouge
- o gris
- o jaune

② The bird is...

Le ballon est ___ et ___ .

- o vert
- o rouge
- o gris
- o jaune
- o bleu

③ The ball is...

L'arbre est ___ et ___ .

- o bleu
- o vert
- o marron
- o orange

④ The tree is...

Le drapeau est ___, ___ et ___ .
(drah·poh)

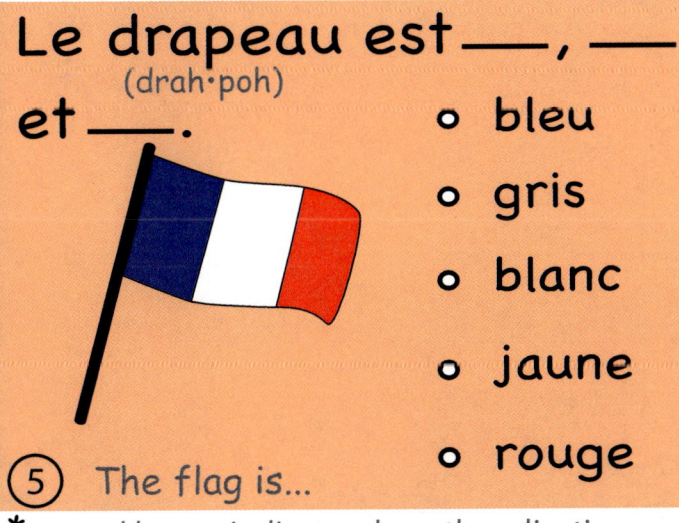

- o bleu
- o gris
- o blanc
- o jaune
- o rouge

⑤ The flag is...

La bille est ___ et ___ .

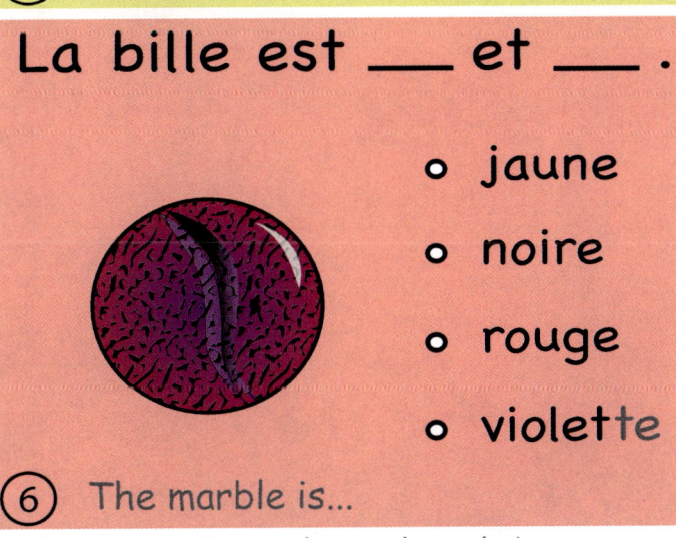

- o jaune
- o noire
- o rouge
- o violette

⑥ The marble is...

* greyed letters indicate where the adjective agree with the noun (in number and gender)   25

SPOT IT

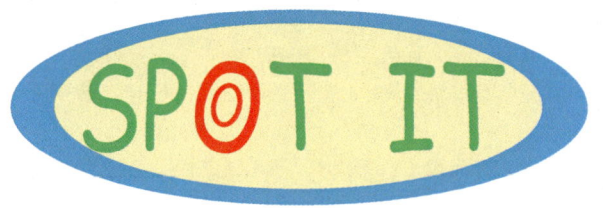

Can you spot these items in the picture ?

DES GRAINES[1]	DES CLEFS	DES FEUILLES	DES RAISINS ET DES MYRTILLES
DES FLEURS	*UNE* ASSIETTE[3]	UN OISEAU	UNE COCCINELLE
UN SCEAU[2]	UN PANIER	DES BILLES	UNE TROTTINETTE
UN BALLON	DES BISCUITS	DES PIERRES	UN ARBRE

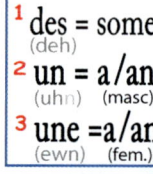

[1] des = some (deh)
[2] un = a/an (uhn) (masc)
[3] une =a/an (ewn) (fem.)

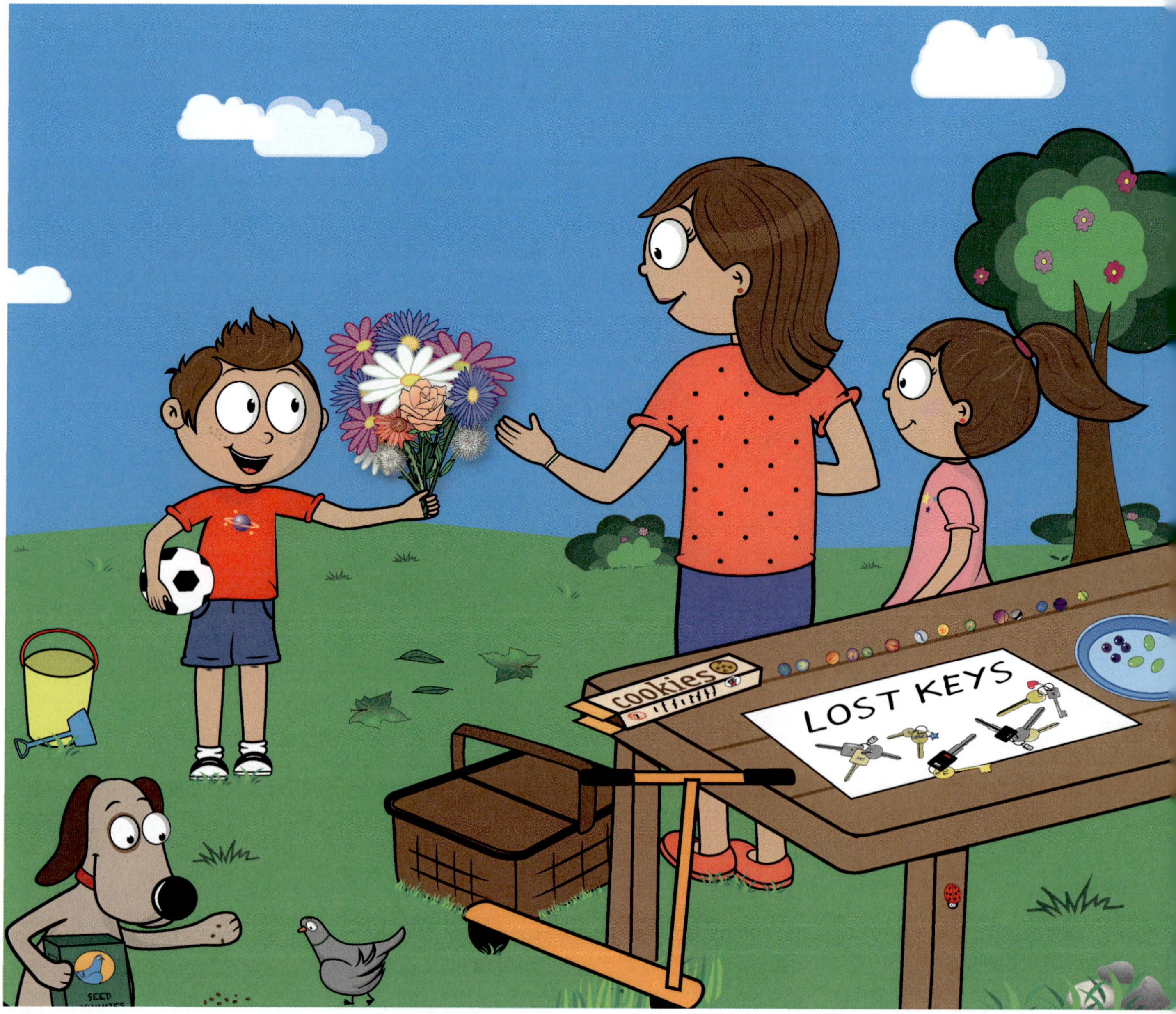

Count by 10

10	DIX dees	**60**	SOIXANTE swah·sahnt
20	VINGT vahn	**70**	SOIXANTE-DIX swah·sahnt·dees
30	TRENTE trahnt	**80**	QUATRE-VINGTS kahtr·vahn
40	QUARANTE kah·rahnt	**90**	QUATRE-VINDT-DIX kah·truh·vahn·dees
50	CINQUANTE sahn-kahnt	**100**	CENT sahn

Count by 100

100 CENT sahn	**600** SIX CENT see sahn
200 DEUX CENT duh sahn	**700** SEPT CENT set sahn
300 TROIS CENT trwah sahn	**800** HUIT CENT wee sahn
400 QUATRE CENT kahtr sahn	**900** NEUF CENT nuhf sahn
500 CINQ CENT sank sahn	**1,000** MILLE meel

Count by 1000

1,000 MILLE (meel)	**6,000** SIX MILLE (see meel)
2,000 DEUX MILLE (duh meel)	**7,000** SEPT MILLE (set meel)
3,000 TROIS MILLE (trwah meel)	**8,000** HUIT MILLE (wee meel)
4,000 QUATRE MILLE (kahtr meel)	**9,000** NEUF MILLE (nuhf meel)
5,000 CINQ MILLE (sank meel)	**10,000** DIX MILLE (dee meel)

Let's mix it up!

21 VINGT-ET-UN (vahn-teh-ahn)	**530** CINQ CENT TRENTE (sank sahn trahnt)
47 QUARANTE-SEPT (kah·rahnt set)	**1,200** MILLE DEUX CENT (meel duh sahn)
68 SOIXANTE-HUIT (swah-sahnt weet)	**735** SEPT CENT TRENTE-CINQ (set saH trahnt sank)
120 CENT VINGT (sahn-vahn)	**2,019** DEUX MILLE DIX-NEUF (duh meel deez nuhf)
10,100 DIX MILLE CENT (dee meel sahn)	**1,000,000** UN MILLION (uhn meel·yohn)

ChatBox

Hello! (hi!)

Bonjour!² bohn-zhoor
(Salut!)¹ sah·lew

My name is ...

Je m'appelle... zhuh mah-pel

I'm ... years old

J'ai ... ans zhay ... ahn

What's your name?

- Comment tu t'appelles?¹
  coh·mahn tew tah·pehl
- Comment vous appellez-vous?²
  coh·mahn voo zah·puh·leh·voo

Yes

Oui wee

No

Non nohn

Please

- S'il te plait¹ seel tuh play
- S'il vous plait² seel voo play

Thank you (very much)

Merci (beaucoup) mehr·see bocoo

You're welcome

De rien duh riahn

How are you doing?

- Comment ça va?¹ / •Ça va?
  coh·mahn sah vah
- Comment allez vous?²
  coh·mahn tah·leh voo

Very good

Très bien treh biahn

Good bye

Au revoir! oh ruh-vwahr

¹ Informal: use it for friends, kids and family   ² Formal: use it for grown-ups you meet, it's more polite

Bonjour!
Je m'appelle Toto, J'ai 8 ans.
Can you tell me your name and your age in French?

NOUNS & ARTICLES

➤ In French, nouns have a gender! They can be either masculine or feminine.
(a noun is a word that represents people, places or things).
It's important for you to know the gender because it determines the article that is used to accompany it. An article is simply the word "the", "a" or "an" as in <u>the</u> dog, <u>a</u> cat, <u>an</u> elephant.

Here are the articles in French:

<u>Definite</u>

le (masc.) **la** (fem.) **les** (plur.)

"the"

<u>Indefinite</u>

un (masc.) **une** (fem.) **des** (plur.)

"a" or "an"   "some"

➤ ## A few pronunciation tips:

The words "un" or "une" can be tricky to pronounce because they sound nasal and the "n" is not always pronounced. So follow this simple rule:

UN : N not pronounced if followed by consonant.   ex: un ballon (uhn bah-lohn)
       N pronounced when followed by a vowel.   ex: un arbre (uhn narbr)
(This: ‿ shows a liaison (lee·eh·zohn), the two words blend into each other and are read as one continuous sound.)

UNE : N <u>always</u> pronounced.

So when you learn a new noun, learn its gender as well. If it's preceded by un or le, it means it's a masculine noun but if you see une or la it's a feminine one.
(Les and Des are used for both fem. and masc. nouns)

➤ The sound of the letter "U" in French does not exist in English but a close description is to purse your lips into a little circle as if to say "OO" (as you do when you whistle) and say "EE" instead. The sound that comes out should be the French "U". Easy!
(It is written as "ew" in our pronunciation guides. eg: - "on" - "sur " (sewr))

French nasal sounds guide

French	Pronunciation symbol	English example (approximately)
-an (as in *le banc*) -en (as in *cent* [100])	-<u>a</u>hn	- p<u>o</u>nd
-un (as in *1* [*un*])	-<u>u</u>hn	she s<u>a</u>ng
-on (as in *le ballon*)	-<u>o</u>hn	- wr<u>o</u>ng (but with lips together as if to whistle /nasal "o")

Build your own flashcard set!

Using flashcards is one of the most effective way to memorize new words.

The next pages contain over 60 flashcards to review, teach and test your child.

Cut along the lines to create your first set. You will find more flashcards in the other Toto & Lola books so you can grow your collection and increase your child's vocabulary.

Cut and use them as is or glue the whole page onto sturdier sheets of paper (or index cards) prior to cutting to create a more durable flashcard set.

Toto & Lola

MY FRENCH FLASHCARDS

0 ZERO	**1** UN	**2** DEUX
3 TROIS	**4** QUATRE	**5** CINQ	**6** SIX
7 SEPT	**8** HUIT	**9** NEUF	**10** DIX
11 ONZE	**12** DOUZE	**13** TREIZE	**14** QUATORZE

FOR CUTTING PURPOSES

15 QUINZE	**16** SEIZE	**17** DIX-SEPT	**18** DIX-HUIT
19 DIX-NEUF	**20** VINGT	**21** VINGT ET UN	**22** VINGT-DEUX
23 VINGT-TROIS	**24** VINGT-QUATRE	**25** VINGT-CINQ	**26** VINGT-SIX
27 VINGT-SEPT	**28** VINGT-HUIT	**29** VINGT-NEUF	**30** TRENTE

FOR CUTTING PURPOSES

BLEU

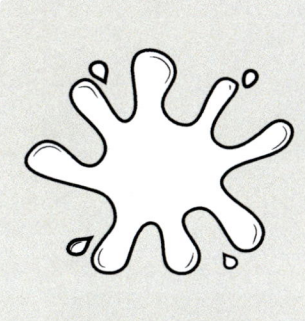

BLANC

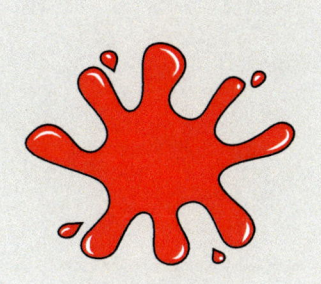

ROUGE

ORANGE

NOIR

VERT

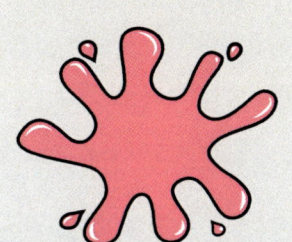

ROSE

MARRON

JAUNE

GRIS

VIOLET

LE BALLON

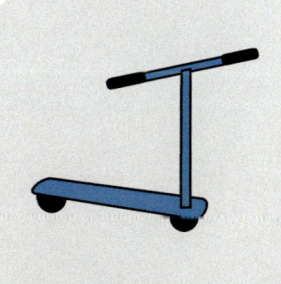

LA TROTTINETTE

LE CHATEAU DE SABLE

LE SCEAU

LA BILLE

FOR CUTTING PURPOSES

L'ARBRE	LA FLEUR	LA COCCINELLE	LA FEUILLE
LA PIERRE	L'OISEAU	LE BANC	LE PANIER
LE DOIGT	LA MYRTILLE	LE RAISIN	LA MAIN
LE BISCUIT	L'ASSIETTE	LA PIÈCE	LA CLEF

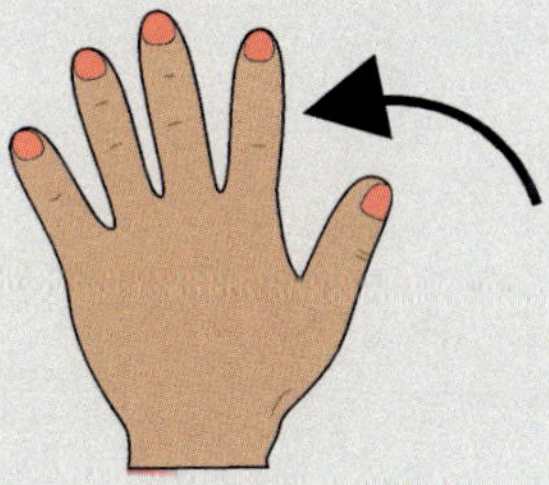

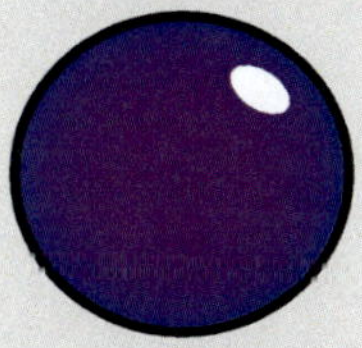

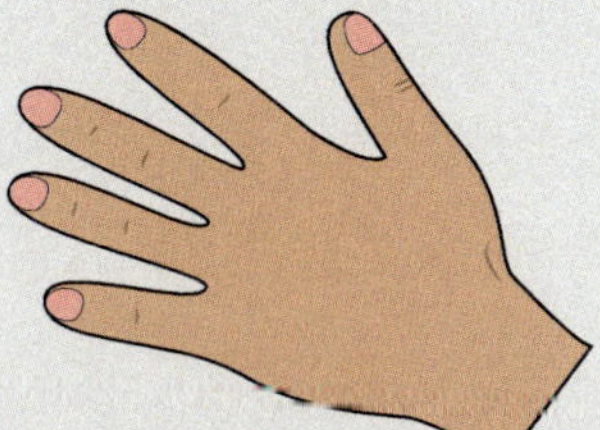

FOR CUTTING PURPOSES

Can you say that in French?

Hello! How are you? (informal)

Very good, thank you!

I found a ball.

I have one key.

I have two cookies.

I eat three fruits

There are four flowers.

I see five birds

I have two hands and ten fingers.

Answers:
Bonjour, Comment ça va? / Salut, Ça va? - Très bien, merci. - J'ai trouvé un ballon. - J'ai une cléf. - J'ai deux biscuits. - Je mange trois fruits. - Il y a quatre fleurs. - Je vois cinq oiseaux. - J'ai deux mains et dix doigts.

THE END

Well done!

Ready for Book 2?

Look for "French with Toto and Lola" on Amazon.com
or lingoboox.com!

Don't forget to visit www.lingoboox.com for free language worksheets
and sign up to be notified when a new book comes out!

Bilingual kids are awesome !

Made in the USA
Monee, IL
16 July 2022

99850774R00026